Dance
of the
Heart

Malthouse African Poetry

Fatima, Habib and Hajja Alkali,	*Secrets of Silence*
Idris Amali,	*Generals without War*
Emevwo Biakolo,	*Strides of the Night*
Emevwo Biakolo,	*Ravages & Solaces*
J. P. Clark,	*A Lot from Paradise*
Gesiere Brisibe-Dorgu,	*Reflections*
Ossie Enekwe,	*Marching to Kilimanjaro*
Harry Garuba,	*Voices from the Fringe*
Taban lo Liyong,	*Homage to Onyame*
Angela Miri,	*Running Waters*
Chimalum Nwankwo,	*Voices of Deep Water*
Silas Obadiah,	*Voices of Silence*
Ezenwa Ohaeto,	*Pieces of Madness*
Tanure Ojaide,	*The Endless Song*
Tanure Ojaide,	*Fate of Vultures & Other Poems*
Tanure Ojaide,	*The Daydream of Ants*
Dike Okoro (ed.)	*Songs for Wonodi*
Dike Okoro (ed.)	*A Long Dream: Poems by Okogbule Wonodi*
Tayo Olafioye,	*Arrowheads to my Heart*
Tayo Olafioye,	*A Stroke of Hope*
Niyi Osundare,	*Waiting Laughters*
Abubakar Othman,	*The Palm of Time*

Dance
of the
Heart

poems by

Dike Okoro

malthouse MP

Malthouse Press Limited

Lagos, Benin, Ibadan, Jos, Port-Harcourt, Zaria

Malthouse Press Limited
43 Onitana Street, Off Stadium Hotel Road
Off Western Avenue, Surulere, Lagos
E-mail: malthouse_press@yahoo.com
malthouse_lagos@yahoo.co.uk
Tel: +234 (01) -773 53 44; 0802 364 2402

First Published 2007
ISBN 978 023 222 2

Dedication

For

Ogboronjo A. Okoro
and
Clara Okoro,
my parents, my heroes

Preface and acknowledgements

Dance of the Heart is a collection of poems bonded by passion and knowledge, and the imaginations it invokes represents the vastness of the human society, pictures of history, tributes to courageous writers, the beauty of landscape, the indebtedness to folklore and oral traditions, and the spontaneity of silent aspirations.

Enriched with poems in a range of styles and from a variety of perspectives, *Dance of the Heart* is organized thematically for aesthetic reasons. The poems in the collection deal with emotions and passions, with a voice that addresses both public and private concerns. Such poems as 'Christopher', 'Arrows', 'To Okogbule Wonodi', 'A Song for Nnamdi' and 'Ode to Akalaka', validate the importance attached to elegies and odes as meaningful literary forms for remembering and celebrating the dead. 'A Song for Nnamdi' is a praise-song/tribute for a deceased in-law and titled Chief from the Niger delta. The diction in this piece, elevated by the careful employment of proverbs, occupies a central place in the cosmic consciousness of the Ogba people of Nigeria's Niger Delta region. 'Ode to Akalaka', another dedication to the dead, is a celebration of history and mythology. Akalaka, in Ogba mythology, is accredited with the founding of the Ogba people and the seventeen groups that make up the Ogba Kingdom. Time and place are dramatized in this piece in order to achieve a certain creative essence. 'Christopher' and 'To Okogbule Wonodi' are both tributes to two of the finest poets of their generation. Both poems experiment with name-calling and the employment of folklore and orating in illustrating traditional African culture. If there is a passionate nostalgia in the reading it is because both poems echo the role of the visionary artist as a repository of memory.

'Niyi Osundare', 'Song for the Bard' and 'Commitment to Song' are tributes to singers/poets. These poems represent a style reminiscent of the West African Griots and Zulu praise singers. They are also vivacious because they are aimed at elevating and celebrating some of Africa's finest and accomplished poets. The poets celebrated here share rare gifts that sustain a visionary place in the cosmic consciousness of the African world. In fact, these poems, though chant-like and musical in beat/movement, illustrate the importance of oral tradition and history. 'Everything Good Will Come,' 'You Will Know Them When You See Them' and 'Dry Your Tears, Homeland,' illustrate emotional attachment to one's homeland. In addition, they are also public declarations of hope for a nation and its citizenry. Other poems in the collection, especially 'For Whom Do We Chant', 'I Know Nothing' and 'Remembering GB', utilize a revolutionary voice that indirectly looks at how history, time, injustice and intellectual space, function in the shaping of a country still in transition.

There are other poems in the collective that merit mention here because they are simple attempts to use names, places, irony of history, and corrupt leadership to establish the relevance of history to the African landscape. Such poems as 'Bonny', 'Isaac Boro Park', 'WS', 'Lament for Claude Ake', 'Rumuigbo,' 'Odi,' 'Wreathe for Vultures' and 'Skies of My Homeland', represent a guarded call and attempt to enlighten readers with important events/individuals that shaped/shape contemporary Nigerian/African society. 'Pardon Granted' is both a reference to historical characters and events that crucial to one's understanding of present day Nigeria. There are names mentioned and references made to resurrect a certain ideal. Dele Giwa, Mamman Vatsa, Ken Saro Wiwa, Obi Wali, and Claude Ake are all political and cultural forces, when put in perspective and remembered in the context of Nigeria's political and cultural history. These icons, though diverse in their callings as statesmen, journalist, activist, military service and scholarship, were all endowed with the power of the pen. Vatsa wrote poems. Giwa was a dynamic editor-in-chief/journalist. Ake wrote books that defined Africa's political/cultural vision and set the foundation for ideas that continue to challenge contemporary African intellectuals and scholars. Wali's challenge to African intellectuals to document their history in their indigenous languages is still a haunting proclamation. Wiwa's place in Nigeria and African history remains a statement for oppressed ethnic groups within and outside the continent. 'WS' is a dedicated to Wole Soyinka. The poem shows and speaks to his importance as both statesman and literary icon for those familiar with his work and vision as a writer.

Idealistically, all the poems in this collection conjure a universal and human vision synonymous with any good work of poetry. Together they construct and open doors of memory where, as I hope, every reader enters to claim, reclaim, question, acknowledge and celebrate the beauty of words dancing. Enjoy.

Dike Okoro
Milwaukee, May 2007

Note:
"At Last," "Remembering GB," "Better luck next time, brother," "I Invite You Enter My Sorrow" first appeared in *Kagablog* (South Africa); "I Know Nothing" appears in *Pindeldyboz* (New York); "Riff from the whirlwind" and "Christopher" will appear in Crossroads, anthology in memory of Christopher Okigbo. "To Okogbule" will/appears in the anthology *Songs for Wonodi*;

Contents

Isaac Boro Park

What is left but the shadow?
Who remembers days
when mothers, daughters,
fathers and sons wiped
their faces, with
drums singing the sun,
praising the rain?
Bus stops knew then
the joy of
youth inspired.
The colors
knew no bounds.
Khaki starched
and pressed, book
bag or slate,
the journey
was earned
in school trips
that fanned
the parent
with delight. And
your flowers,
they kept
lovers coming
to steal a
moment or two,
a toast to
adulthood calling.
But your face
is now
the sorry tale.
Fence broken,
bushes all over;
brick here and

there.
No children
to chase paper
kites under
your watch.
Is this the promise?
A name left
to where

memory last visited
cannot be recalled.

*Isaac Boro: Ijaw/Niger Delta visionary leader and Major during the Nigerian Civil War. He was later betrayed and killed by hired commandos.

*Isaac Boro Park: Once notable flower garden, recreation ground, and park in Port Harcourt, named after the late Major Isaac Adaka Boro. Today the park remains a shadow of what it once stood for.

The flavour of heritage

I brushed the cheek of dawn today,
hungry for mackerel smoked and
soaked in red pepper and palm oil.
No show or place for the fork,
just hands feeling and dipping
to journey down throat
the flavor of heritage passed down.
This is PH, my brother,
Garden City now *na wa o* city.
The flowers and trees are gone,
but not the memories that hang
while dreams still walk and chase.
Motorcycles know no bounds here.
Cars and trailers aim for the sky
on the express way, where
hawkers sing their faith
sealed in how much
the pocket holds or takes home.
My friend, my brother, *na wa o,*
this our country self. Na wetin
man pikin go do now?
The eyes must look straight here,
to track the sight of all around.
No water passes through a gutter
without a stop and go here.
This is Garden City,
where the warden's spike
frightens the prison mice
and the executioner's faint steps
steal sleep
in the eyes of the prisoner
on death row.
This is the city
where Saro's song

shook the sky
and wonders
stumbled speech
in the mouth of time.
And the rivers

still mourn,
dirge
for the broken
song
an epitaph
in riddles.

NPA

Another acronym for
Never Plan Ahead.
This is no joke.
The structure hangs
like a cobweb
waiting to be
scraped by a broom.
What use
do they have
for memory
here? All they
speak of is
the next buyout
or sale of
what remains of
the once prized bride.
That's the
state of NPA.
No more ships
painting the dock
with ballads
of Europe and
Asia's finest
products
and rejects
regularly.
At least
that's gone,
for today
rings of
whatever comes.
Whenever it comes
we shall take
and keep,
cargo containers.

The seasons
were great
while they lasted.
The morning
will grow

with fanfares
forgotten,
but not
the sun
hanging
over
what is left
of the
Sea port
once
Ocean terminal.

Presidential Hotel

They are the last of the money hawkers.
They flee on foot they work in groups.
Dollars and pounds they have,
nairas in millions they house.
Stacks of crates
under mystery safes
only the trusted know.
The robbers stay away.
Who blames the snake
for keeping away from the tortoise?
Young and old,
the song they sing
is the same.
Old cars, brand
new cars,
jeeps,
motorcycles,
your foreign currency
is what counts.
The sheds are there.
The eyes are watching,
under skies made safe by dawn
and circumstances
detailing fate and support.
They stalk the car windows.
They look out for eyes calling.
They watch their backs for safety's sake,
in a profession driven by passion
in a country full of survival stories.

You will know them when you see them

They are the relatives and elders you left behind.
They are the young ones who were still feeding on the breast
when your legend stood like the *iroko* on the streets
and your peers honored you with praise names.
This is the tale of the traveling son,
this is the song of the area boy,
this is the memory of the time-inspired,
the ones who left home
in search of the flag flying in foreign soil.
Some came back themselves,
some came back with selves.
And the churches drowned in mothers' cries and
widows' songs.
Blame the jealous uncle in the village
for taking out his anger
at the request of the herbalist.
Nobody remembered
to bring him common sweet
from the paradise many flood the airports yearly
to stalk and walk, he cried.
Blame the auntie
now a forgotten wind chime.
At least nobody thinks of the past now.
Today matters most
and tomorrow even more.
Such is the tale of the returning son,
the one whose smile lights the dark
in hearts deluged by frustration
in the homeland.
The one whose laugh
is enough to speed up
the healing of one caught by malaria.

Send him to the village
and his presence
is a gathering of voices.
Faces he remembers,
faces strange,
faces begging for recognition.
He is bound
to embrace all.
They sang him good luck
the day the passport
was stamped
to seal his place
in their warmth and prayers.
Today, they too
will now sing him welcome,
waiting on his gifts
to water the flowers of the heart.

Dry your eyes, homeland

I was the deflated tyre
on the highroad to *e go betta*[*] country.
The eagle knows my eyes,
having dined with me
the day the ocean dried and
the sun cried blues.

I was the deflated tyre
on Shagamu express way.
All buses to and from
the market called Lagos
know my face.
A blind man can tell you
my voice.
The unborn will sing you
my heartache.

But my muted ode
will break out
in the rubble,
when tomorrow cracks open
our triple heritage.

---

[*] Pidgin English - "It will be better."

Bonny

Song of the new season,
Oil rubbing the face of the sun,
Industrial landscape floating on sea.
Did I hear the leper say
your warmth is paradise?
The car robber dreads your presence
because the rat has no hole to hide in your wake.
The tourist keeps asking for more of you
because you remind him of the horizon
that blesses hearts with the songs of
a Caribbean dawn.
Palm tree, coconut tree, beach sand.
So fresh, so alluring.
Blue sky, seashore whispers.
Residents with eyes talking, singing
of love's warmth and sorrow.
A king for his people
rules here. Evidence
of Jaja's legacy
and the presence of the forefathers.
Ships resting ashore, boats flying
under the sun, fishermen
busy with hook.
And the joy of walking on bare feet,
a delight to the little ones
Soccer crazy and play ready,
leaving in the sun
shadows of their dances.

Odi

Termites will always
find a home in the wet wood.
Can the massacre of your beloved
be erased from memory?
The sky saw, the river heard
the rage of the bullets, the
crack of the whip, the
blow of the bayonet
and the fury of the heavy boots.
Was the bloodied face, the
cracked rib, the dripping nose
and the elders' songs
wind chimes forgotten?
Your fate was sealed
in the twisted irony of time.
While the world stood in awe,
you swallowed your sorrow
without a grain of wheat
from the sacred chaff.

The marketplace

They say it is empty,
but I can hear a bird singing.
Of what it sings
I dare not ask.
Some songs are meant
to be heard,
others to be devoured,
like the moon's beam
which comes with
the crickets' chirrup.
Such an amazing anthem
for reflections much ado,
like the sun's ray,
a billion voices
in one light.
Some argue
these are the unborn
forewarning us
of their coming,
the precious moments
we eagerly await
to sow
another seed of salvation.
What will the torchbearers
say then, when theirs
is a light that quenches
and the sun's is the occasional singer
whose stay is daily?
And the heart of the marketplace
knows this. Voices dread
their ears, a telling revelation of
the barren's cry and
the deaf's vow. Nothing is
empty but that which

accepts it is.
This is not an ordinary
song. This is
the heartbeat
of the marketplace.

For thirty days

For thirty days
a strong wind kissed
my home at night.
It turned into a woman
on the fortieth day
and sang to me
of tales of warriors
and why the
moon betrayed
the sun.
Each time I
tried to ask
a question,
the silence
so heavy
withstood
my fire
and pressed
me to sing
more, more
to the voice of origin.
Then, one day,
when the night
had failed
to hold the river back,
I entered
the womb of the waters.
There and then,
the tales, the warriors
and the wind
laughed and laughed
till I asked
what all the laughing
was for.
And they said
a strong wind
lives inside of me.

Christopher

Wait for me at Ojoto,
you holding a gourd
and a throat full of songs.
When I'm rid of
the spoils of the day,
arrest me
with lofty words
coined for
Idoto's warrior poet.

What compels
the palm tree to dance?
What presses
the *iroko* for praise?
There's a canoe
shooting on high sea;
the wind's its paddler.
A sparrow on pierced wings
stands on a rock,
dirging
from beak tireless.
Up in the sky,
a palm is open.
It reads a call for song.
I shall sing a song.
Not for my delight
but of your plight,
Echo in the palm grove,
Oil that never fades,
Dew that never dries,
Water nourishing the coconut,
Feet that keep alive
the town's square,
town crier whose gong is

the dance of the pregnant mother.
Where have you been, where
have you gone to?
What did the palm fronds say
upon your arrival before the forefathers,
watcher of Heavensgate,
flute player in season of agony,
eye that stayed open when all others were asleep?
You sang of the battered elephant,
long before the bushes wrote its elegy.
You prepared the way for thunder's coming,
even before our ears learned of its rage.
Nwa ji re ehe na aka abia uwa[*]
What did we learn from your riddled palm?

---

[*] Igbo for child who came to the world with a mission

Arrows

Okute is gone.
A late sun
brought news
of his mission
to the marketplace.
Hurry me a keg,
this throat is thirsty.
What shall we
say
of the brave
who left
the grieving
to torrents of sorrow.
Was his departure to be
an excursion,
this day
will not be summoned
to the spate of elegies.
You, draped
in beads and head
full of tributes,
lead the procession
round the casket.
Let eyes watching
learn from
the ways of the sun
and compose
songs for the moon.
The head will always
be carried by the body.
We saw the brave heart
at work
in the morning of youth,
whilst burdened

by the weight of responsibility.
Not a tear spattered
from eyes focused on the sky.
His heels knew
the urgency of statements.
He conducted himself
under the doctrine of
terms fertile.
But there's a story
to the ways of the whirlwind.
We know that
because we see that today
as we sit,
arms folded;
as we stand,
hand to cheek,
elbow supported by
arms across chest,
believing there's
a dance in a place
where the brave, the
learned, the loved
and the grieving
shall all meet
to raise high
this question
of love's endless
journey.

Commitment to song

Got to make it,
stalking the shadows
of the elders.
Feather in hat,
goat horn steady
within grasp,
this day deserves praise.
Praises are deserving
of they who woke
at dawn
to stalk the sun
with stories
compelling the
forefathers to tears.
Hand to brow,
leg crossed,
let me wait on the keg
as I serve praises
to the opulent skies.

Tanure,[*] what rifled your heart
to press Aridon[**] to
bring back your wealth
from rogue vaults?
Niyi,[+] Ikere[++] must be
proud
your revelation
in the eye of the earth

---

[*] Tanure: reference here is to Tanure Ojaide, the renowned Nigerian scholar/poet/editor and winner of the Commonwealth/All Africa Christopher Okigbo poetry prize

[**] Aridon: memory god in Ojaide's Urhobo ethnic Urhobo mythology

[+] Niyi: reference here is to the Nigerian and Noma Award for Africa winning poet and scholar, Niyi Osundare

[++] Ikere: Osundare's hometown

still frightens the tortoise.
Frank,[♣] Likoma[♣♣]
has not known a better
songster.
Lupenga,[*] the veldts
still listen to the crackle at midnight.

Chimalum,[a]
I have heard the cry
from the womb in the heart.
All roads confess
the foul play of the ages.
Do we need a blind man
to tell us what Mazisi[b] deserves?
Ironies are meant
for geniuses.
The dew shall
come and go,
yet the grass
shall retain its legends.
I have known one too.
He came
like a fine melody
accompanying
the morning ray.
Fears gathered
to hail his tracks.
Whatever happened, Oguibe?[c]
There are hearts
still lamenting your break.

♣ Reference here is to Frank Chipasula, renowned editor of major Southern African/African Women poetry collections and poet

♣♣ Likoma: Chipasula's hometown

* Malawian poet/scholar resident in the USA

a Chimalum Nwankwo, Nigerian poet resident in the USA

b The accomplished Zulu historian/poet/scholar and South African poet laureate, Mazisi Kunene

c Olu Oguibe, renowned artist/poet/scholar resident in the USA and winner of the 1992 All Africa Christopher Okigbo prize for poetry

And you, Motsapi,[d]
I step the earth tenderly
these days,
knowing the ocean is very shallow,
not trusting
neon nights draped in blue funk,
for the sun
still rises in the east
and tongues
tire not
from evicting
a word or two
for Acoli's singer.
Okot,[e] how many

lines did you cut
to entice ears
with Lawino's song?
Wangusa,[f] we
know why
the tetrarch of the jungle
is a rare sight these days,
its tusk an endangered treasure.
Song, you came to me
and my heart
is still reveling from
your shadows and
those untracked,
even as the sun leaves
to rise another day.

---

[d] One of South Africa's highly acclaimed and anthologized poets
[e] The famous Uganda scholar/poet, Okot p'Bitek
[f] Timothy Wangusa, scholar/poet/fiction writer from Uganda

Song for the bard

And you, Tanure,
where the rain muddied the red soil
it gave you the river and a canoe.

Orator on endless spree.
Moonraider who evades the hag
To paint nights in distant lands.

Pride of FGC-Warri.
Urhobo's music connoisseur.
Strange lands called
and he surveyed,
leaving behind
verses of diamond.

Wordsmith who shunned
the wait at the smithy
to color skies
with words.

Charlotte's adopted sun
whose vision spurned
the eagles' mission.

Where there is a peacock
there's a dance.
He who sang the songs of songs
while waiting on the song of songs.

Minstrel the forefathers gifted
with three eyes.

Twirling dust assaulted him
from roads untarred,

yet he walked away
lighting like mirages
glistening.

He who covered words
in native chalk and
composed themes
from human light
to serve wisdom
in the womb of the calabash.
And they swore
it was served
in a half calabash.

For you, I spill this gourd,
that the morning sun
may spill mine too,
amidst the clamor
of drums
and the gyroscope
of rising crowds.

Notes : FGC-Warri: Government owned high school attended by the poet.
Urhobo: the poet's hometown
The italicized lines are taken from a short story *Worlds That Flourish* by Ben Okri.

Wreath for vultures

Broom within grasp,
who will reach
for the dirt of the land?
There's a vulture
atop the treasured tree.
Do not ask me
what it stands waiting
for.
Its kind hover the sky.
They wait on the
old game they know best.
Mothers pray
to the ray at noon.
At least there shall be
dusk to assure them dawn.
Every land has seen
its golden name turn rusty.
This shall not be an exception.
In the streets,
arbiters of agony take turns
swinging at the pipe players, smiling
for every sorrow inflicted.
They shall eat grass,
sitting on the bench of their exhaustion.
Pity the wicked,
pity the wily,
their elegies already flood
the eye of the earth.
And when they're lowered
only their kind wipes tears
from eyes alien to vision.

Salutation

Dry leaves carpet the roads, and
dust clouds serenade the afternoons.
The bald headed ambusher flaps
from treetop beyond reach.
This sun too has seen the madness turn earnest, even
when it rains to bless the days with songs endless.

Pardon granted

Today I stand
by headstones.
No eulogies celebrate
the unknown soldier.
But I hold no rifle,
as this heart pounds
with no trifle.
It is the spirit
of the forgotten
that I have come
to sing.
Vatsa,[♣]
the pen has never slept
since cowards
dragged you
to the dark pit.
Giwa,[♥]
a name may mean
a thousand things in letters,
yet no word in print
qualifies your bravery.
Ake,[♠]
you see the trouble with name calling, don't you?
the grass is still dry
since the lagoon in Lagos
robbed us of your promise.

[♣] One of Nigeria's best-loved soldier-poet accused and executed with other Generals in 1986, following allegations of their involvement in a coup plot to overthrow the then military junta

[♥] Dele Giwa, founding Editor-in-Chief of *Newswatch* magazine who was a victim of a letter bomb on October 19, 1986

[♠] Claude Ake, renowned social scientist and international scholar from Omoku in Nigeria's Niger Delta region who died in a plane crash in Lagos on November 7, 1996

Wiwa,[♦]
I think I could be
silent over your epic,
if only for once
memory can recover
the legends of your topics
the world's newspapers
found too graphic for pages.

Wali,[♪]
only in the homeland
with so much promise
are heroes forgotten.
I shall sing your absence
with silence,
not ashamed to drape
myself in green and white.
For I know one thing
about the sun:
it may die today,
yet it shall
live another day.

[♦] Ogoni martyr, poet, fiction writer and environmentalist from Nigeria's Niger Delta region. Hung with 8 other Ogoni freedom fighters on November 10, 1995

[♪] Obi Wali, critic, literary scholar and political freedom fighter from Nigeria's Niger Delta region who was murdered in home on 6th April, 1993

Better luck next time, brother

The wind warned you, yet you
challenged it to a senseless race.

The river read you your rights,
yet you pester it with questions.

The sun showed you
the many scars the living
inflict on love, and you
never cared to ask why.

The rain brought you
tears to celebrate
the burial of your umbilical cord,
and you took it for granted.

The moon taught you
to watch and pray,
yet you accuse it of conspiracy.

Better luck next time, brother.
Hope you learn, after the storm.

To Okogbule Wonodi

The Sun has faded.
Let the mourning begin.
Who lights now the first light
to open ancient doors,
ushering in praises
from arcane regions
walked by bards?
Who brings now
the gourd of honor
to spill a libation for Wonodi,
let him do so,
gifting wings
to minds present,
for we are here
to sing the dead
who are alive in our words
and to restore
the place of he who is like palm oil
to family and ancestors.

Wonodi,
as this sun sets
so sets
your limits
now one with
the crisscrossing moon.
With your memory
we wash this moment
to place
the marble of respect.
Who denies the elephant its place
in the legend of the grass?

Who says the weaverbird
has no song
when its song
is an anthem
in distant lands?
But to every song
there is an end.
So let us leave

this moment,
painting the moon
with what we
know best by mouth.
Knowing yet
that we remember
he who walked
this path
but is now
with the sun.

Afrobeat party

(for Ikwunga Wonodi & Ogugua Iwelu)

Ikwunga has taken the microphone.
Eyes rise with the tilt of expectation.
Wonodi's son stands before us
to feed hearts starving with
the wisdom of the ancestors.
Let him be encouraged by
our claps and nods.
Every singer is deserving of reassurance
from a listening audience.
What he creates from passion ageless,
that we must embrace
with attention unreserved.
Let the jeers keep on,
and the cheers too.
The long night
so full of gong rights
shall be ours to claim.
The plate is passed around;
there is life in the kola nut.

Ogugua has taken the microphone.
This spotlight is deserving of Iwelu's son too.
Let him be showered with greetings fair;
our ears shall not fail him.
There's a coalescing beyond beats & drums,
when people singing the rainbow are
enjoined in one parlor.
There's more in blood
than the eyes can see.
It is true

night has more ways
to please the spirit
than light can see.
So let us begin
where the speaking ends.
Among the subtleties
of plates loaded
and cups frothing.

A song for Nnamdi[♥]

An uneventful day
will not invite
the gathering of legs
that ring the casket
to spill praises
for whom we are quietly gathered.

Nnamdi, words deny you now
but they shall court your name
long after you are lowered
to fulfill the calling
of your maker.

Brave heart that dared
thunder to bark
like the lion's roar;
brave bird that flew
to dare heights
when the sky mocked
the winged.

I was caught
in the lust for archery
in a distant land,
when a telegram
posted the unexpected news.

So it was you
who told me in my sleep
that thirteen years
away from mother's cradle
is enough to fly home.

[♥] In memory of Chief Nnamdi Osademe, a prominent community builder and political think-tank from Ogbaland/Niger Delta who died young at age 42.

Brother, I didn't know
you'll be called to
the dance of the woodchoppers
so soon.

In-law, your journey on the canoe
may steal you from our eyes,
but will never swallow
the glow you left in our hearts.

Nnamdi, I want to cry.
But I will disrobe the sky if I do.
Nnamdi, I want to kneel.
Yet the earth trembles from
my intentions.
Nnamdi, let me better yet
pause at the smile on your face,
for there is a call more urgent than ours
in need of your gifts.

Rumuigbo[*]

Fourteen years removed
from the thunderstorm
that silenced your womb,
Obi Wali's macheting.
Today your face is
a marketplace
where eyes meet
to detect what ails
the belly with songs
and what lends
dance to the restless
at your roundabout,
where the coming
and the going
circle to get to their end,
and faces pay tribute
to the native son
whose confession
rocked the
intellectual house
at Makerere
five decades back.
Today,
his walking stick,
his fitted hat,
his sprawling gown
and famed shoes

---

[*] Home town of Obi Wali. Nigerian scholar and statesman whose article published in Transition number 10 and presented at the 1962 African writers conference at Makerere University in Uganda challenged African writers to write in their indigenous languages. He was a victim of assassination in his home in 1993.

speak to observers
what remains of
this sun of the land
now its memory of
the times.

Song for the traveller

You carry the village with you.
Wherever you leave a footprint
has been home to you.
The sun will not rise to ruminate
your betrayal.
Nor will the sky mourn your trial.
In your heart lie
the songs of the deserted.
And in your eyes live
the drums of the remembered.
But isn't the bone still naked
though clothed by flesh?
Let your voice be the bride of
the ears of the marketplace.
You'll return
after learning from the sun
that the only way home
is not the ray leading you into new dawns,
but the shadow stalking you.

Niyi Osundare

Ikere's[♣] sun,
delight us with your light.
Olosunta's[♠] conjurer,
catapult us
into the womb of
your sacred calabash.
A farmer once harvested,
late in the afternoon,
the rewards of patience
to take home
the generosity of the soil.
You were the meticulous one
from the onset,
when your rays
torn from the cheek of
an adventurous sky,
brought you a King's ransom
before midlife.
The elder who listens
and speaks not a word
in the presence of the young,
is a treasure box.
Finer days we have known
plucking your verse;
brighter moments we have lived
singing your legacy.
Let the proud eagle
standing on Olumo
spread its large wings now.
The sun shall not deny its talons.
Nor shall the wind deny its beak
and eyes, the fortune of daylight.

[♣] Niyi Osundare's hometown of Ikere Ekiti
[♠] Rock outcrop in the poet's hometown

Onye-isike

Even you, we thought you knew better.
We gave you a horsetail and
concubines to attend to your desires,
called you by praise names
in the public place
to stamp your name and fame
in the legend of our time.
But you have proved to us
why the modest one who
retreats to its carapace
cannot be trusted.
Did we not sing you a song in the sun?
Did we not wipe your dirt with the rain?
Yet you return our favors
with eyes sharper than arrows,
leaving scars in our minds
that cannot be healed.
How sad to learn that
in them that we place a crown
we are bound to our own regrets
in hours of silence.
You promised to raise in the homestead
a gathering steady with joy
and a dream flowing with
the promise of a stream.
But what the heart thinks
is not always what the eyes see.
Away now, with your faulty footsteps.
We do not need the sorrow bred
from your smile anymore.
We thought you knew better.
You now a mere shadow of
the one entrusted with a horsetail
and praise names in public.

Nonye

Village dame.
Talking to her is like
trying to retrieve water
from a well so hollow it
evades the rope-assisted
bucket.
Ask the village lads
why they turn their necks
when the sun brings
her out in the morning,
or why they talk of money
and the quest for fame
when she opens and closes
the door of a brand new
Mercedes Benz
or a Hummer to their
sighs and silences.
Nonye is the village dame.
It does not take the wisdom
of Solomon to sort through
her face to know her ilk,
because the sun never lies.

Lament for Claude Ake[•]

Ants are raiding the felled tree.
The Iroko lies naked before parasites.

My brother and my kinsman,
your shadow will never be an orphan in our minds.

Like the cockcrow that reminds the farmers of
their ritual rise and walk
to sharpen cutlass and wear their work dress,
like the river song that compel fishermen
to hurry net, basket, worms and hooks
to the floating canoe and waterside,
our memories of you shall remain a stream in our veins,
through rain and sun,
as we speak of your song
that welcomed many a bird
at the gathering of minds wise from the thirst for knowledge.
You, member of the masters of the academy,
you, painter of Africa's fears with dreams,
you, fiery one with speeches compelling scholars
to sleepless days and moments of wonderment
in places distant and near,
sleep well, even now that inaction illustrates your voice.

A river may be rid of song
when the tide is silent,
but every navigator carries
in their heart
the drumbeats of its waves.

We see many with the same drumbeats,

[•] Claude Ake: erstwhile professor of political science at Yale University/USA & renowned Nigerian/African scholar and social scientist from Omoku, Ogbaland, Nigeria. He died in a plane crash in Lagos in 1997.

singing in daylight
at the market square in Omoku,
where old men and women praise your legend
in broken kola nut and talks of
them who read to raise the shoulder of the village.
But are words spoken enough to restore dignity to heroes
forgotten?
Time vanishes, days melt.
From the suspicious footprints of the sun
farmlands grow and glow from
the sacrifice of arms and legs.
Cars and motorcycles break and
head on to secret ends,
through August rain and December harmattan.
But you, my kinsman,
I shall raise a cup for you
at the festival ground
where young maidens swing their waists
and young men watch
with eyes lit, and arms criss-crossed.
I shall speak of your guns and runs
in the hollow sepulcher of decades
now asleep in memory's vessel
and the naked silence of the gatherers
who do not remember the songs of the felled *iroko.*
Your death shall be my comforter,
even in the homeland
where you are not remembered.
And in far away Harare,
where your kinsmen decline your war songs
In their roll call,
I shall preserve for you
a song that death cannot snatch,
like the robe of dignity now worn for you
by America's Ford Foundation.

Mindbug

There's nothing
in the sky.
Spare your neck
the labor of
curiosity.
A dream is but
an imagination.
You only fly
to the clouds
the dance
of your eyes.
And the trust
of the ground
on which
you stand
is only
measured
by the
wisdom of
your feet.
Learn to
read the wind.
Listen more
often
to birds
and crickets
There's magic
in their language,
and the stories
they sing
color the skies
with promises
unborn.

Remembering

for Port Harcourt

How do I explain to my son
that I lied when I told him
our skies are blue, rich and golden
with beauty beyond the imagination of tourists?
What do I say to my daughter
who worries me everyday to
take her to the land of my birth,
that south coastal town overlooking the Atlantic,
a stone throw from the bight of Guinea?
These are days when news from
the Niger delta is weighty
to the heart and memory nibs
at one's conscience when one catches
a glimpse of residents washing in
and drinking from mud-colored water and
fighting for space in rusty buses overloaded
with passengers and the bus driver
and conductor hardly in the mood
for a smile or joke and
the job-hunting graduate,
credentials tucked under armpit,
waits in line for the next bus ride
sweating, himself a story
begging for a reader
as oil workers and politicians
shoot for home
on brand new jeeps and cars loaded with
bottled Spring Water,
nodding to thumping music
in AC heaven and leathered cushions,
ironies wired online via BBC or CNN.
And the heart immediately jumps,
abandons the allurement of the present,

this honey-coated world of the privileged
where one easily forgets
that far away in places remembered occasionally
and unknown to folks here,
eyes leached to the sky are heavy with water and
folded arms compel the sun to tears,
for a place once decorated with
mango and guava trees,
buildings erected and tagged GRA
with verandas and villas
modeled on architecture reminiscent
of Europe's finest,
a place where the golf course awaited
the wealthy and the sport-minded
on weekends and weekdays,
sight of the caddie dragging along
after the golfer at Ernest Ikoli Street,
a place where every street
had trees and flowers
ambushed by multicolored
birds that have since become
part of the burden biting memory
now that the sun beats folks
and there's hardly a shed to take refuge.
This is no imitation of art.
This is how the traveler chats with lamentation
to remember home that is far away from home.

Skies of my homeland

Skies of my homeland,
I greet you.
Radiance of my striding feet,
the returning son sings your praise.
There are potholes,
there are red soils,
there are dagger eyes,
but your love
remains the same.
You who breathe in the goat slaughtered, roasted and scraped
before the washing and the cutting;
you who encourage the believing trader
even when the marketers are few
and he plants his buttocks on chair,
hand holding his chin,
looking out for the lucky face,
yet knowing the sun is never late
to spare the pockets
the blues of emptiness.
You, witness to the vendors' song,
bare feet, everyday
up the bridge,
down the streets,
as the beat goes on.
You, comforter of
the hardworking mother,
baby strapped to her back,
yet she sits by the roadside,
fanning the roasting corn and pear
in the May night while
sorting through old newspapers
to wrap the patient customers' buy.
You, mournful watcher
of the troubled youth who betrays

the walls of the classroom
for love of cult and villainy,
and yet misunderstood
by the driving forces
dictating the times,
where hope is a kite
cutting through
Skies opulent.

At last

It was not because I enjoyed your dance
that I have come back to watch you by chance.

It was not because I killed your charm
that I have come to decry its harm.

It was because I could no longer get up
and run to the field before the first cockcrow.

It was because no matter what was said
we knew we were bound to renew the light of days gone.

It was, it was, it was, and I mean it, the things
we did not do, or even knew of…

I invite you to enter my sorrow

I invite you to enter my sorrow,
if you have a heart that's never felt
the weight of agony fraught with penury.
A hen, feathers beaten by empathy,
crying to the open skies
for its chick taken to the sacrificial tree branch
by a kite, knows
the elephant homing in my silence more than you do.
A mother antelope that watches
a pack of lions tear apart its newborn
shares the burden of my fallen head.
Do not offer me a cup of wine
to end the drought in my throat.
Do not whisper to my ears
your worldly drums of elevation.
I have swam in the stream home to the dreaded python.
my eyes are wise like an owl's at night.
My legs lighter than a leopard's when an elephant draws near.
Come to me, you whose heart
knows nothing of scars from a talon
And tell me what you see.

And we took home his words

Obiakor brought home the drought last night.
The elders warned that a man who has fought
a ghost in the bush of strange spirits ought not
be left alone to ponder his fate when the eyes
of the caring shield him from his fears.
You should see him, feet heavy from
the elephant he carried in his head.
You should hear him then, words rushing
like the waterfall, and body shaking
like the tree forced to dance by an intruding wind.
What he did not say, we knew he meant to.
What he said, we agreed he had to.
Arms folded, eyes restless, ears attentive,
we took home his words, not because we cared
but because we dared the tormentors of his mind
and wished for a date with their spells.
But a wise mind, like the old would say, never
goes to war against the enemy it knows might defeat him.
He only sees reason in the evasion of danger
to spare the living the anger of the dead
who, if they knew in advance, would not avoid
the takers of their shadows and glows.
So let us leave Obiakor to his raving.
At least we know with him came the drought.
And we saw it off, agreeing that the one who brought to us
fear
is now a leaf spared the wrath of locusts!

When nature rids me of the vigour of youth

Leave me with the children
under the mango tree
while the sun shines over us.
Do not bring to my nose
the tyrant's fart
from the leathered cushions
of his dignified palace,
for my nose is no stranger
to the glory of the stench considered elegant.
Let me be with the young ones
whose eyes shall see
the specter of the new dawn.
Leave me with them,
for I have a thousand songs
to sing to their noble hearts.
As for the fraudsters and the
illegal tax collectors,
keep them away from my shadow.
I have paid my levies and taxies
with the song of the unemployed
graduate nobody heard of.
I have written my sorrow
on the face of the sky,
when the ears of tomorrow
would not listen to the tussle and
hassle in the space I occupy.
And for you, Mr. Politician,
when that day comes
and your rotten teeth defy
all applicable laws of modern technology,
remember the old man under
the generous mango tree.
Do not deny his voice then
the ears of the marketplace.

You will know the executioners of your dream

You will know the executioners of your dream
by the tracks of their laughter.
They paint the sacred mask with the flames of their lust,
and the hills and valleys of the homeland grieve
from the heartless circus play of their dreadful passion.
Who will stand in their way to make them turn their necks
and refrain from their ways that hurry the blind
down streets and alleys where the use for the eyes
of the trusted one is no longer a necessity?
Who will remind them that to every impostor
there is a rainy day waiting to reveal to them
the balance in nature's order?
They sit and watch their victims, excited
at the tormented ones' cry and rage.
They sip and drink to the full, ignoring
the shouts and heartaches that color the streets
with silence and violence, all because
the malaise is beyond their doorstep.
The bulletproof cars and vehicles will not
spare them the stench of their feces,
when the moon delays the coming of the sun
to torture them with the dance of the wind.
You will know the executioners of your dream
by the tracks of their laughter,
not by the tears they leave on faces
shut out of their memory and worry.

Save the long talk for another occasion, Sir

Save the long talk for another occasion, Sir.
That I have come to ask for your daughter's
hand in marriage is enough.
I did not bring a trailer load of yams
and the fattened calf you demanded in my absence.
But I know one thing I can guarantee
you who still live in a world pushed to the wall
by the tormentors of your imagination.
You want a son-in-law who will present to you
a car and a bride price you will sing to your grave.
You want a young man who will write your name
on the sky, so the city's legend will not be complete
without the mention of you and your family.
Relax, Sir, happiness is not an item in the market.
You can only earn it when you have tasted
of the bitterness of abandoning your self
for the advancement of others.
That's when you can sit back and look,
without delusion, at the mirror standing
before you, the replica of tomorrow
you now chide, without conscientiously
thinking of your daughter's sake and
the singer who has come to win
her hand to the great dance.

WS

you loaned the world your dance so
yinka may be joined in holy matrimony
with the roll call at Olympus.

Ake's marble of diamond;
effigy of lust in terrains distant.

book of poems robbing bullies of sleep.
strainer whose feet are no stranger
to troubled shores.

our garment of countless holes
long your stitching speech.

who says the poet has no say
in the affairs of the state?

Idanre's piper homeward outward bound.
eagle whose vision leashes eyes to stars.

they say the child that robs its mother of
sleep shall have no sleep.

carry on with your cry for the distressed mother.
her children are not deserving of
the stress visited on them by circumstance.

I only know of hands

I know nothing about exile
or apparitions that arrest the heart.
Call me when you find
the lonely canoe. I only know of hands,
not names.

This too is forgiveness

Love the dog that bit you
in the sun. Study carefully
its scars in the rain.
The moon will wash your pain
when it comes out to lick
the dog's howling out of the air.
This too is forgiveness.

I know nothing

I know nothing
of love that hates.
See the tree
in the sky. Do you
know of its loneliness?
Hear
its cry for company?
Tell the sparrow your riddle,
sing to it
your thirst that's sky bound.
There, there
in your voice
lies the perching
the tree waits for.

The moon is out

Let me dance tonight,
with the limbs of a sacred moon
the bangles cast round my ankles.
Let me dance tonight, for the sun
that drank the goat's blood
to charm the boastful earth. Are joys
not amulets sprouted from the dancer's vein?

Everything good will come

Sefi was right!
Everything good will come.
I have looked at the sun
and do not blame it for being late.
I have listened to the rain
and there are secrets untapped
in its drops.
You can tell from the
silences in our midst
that the present
is a dangerous place to live,
and the fruits of roots
sustaining our soil
have not been nutritious
like the fruits of years past.
But the times have always
been sandstones
on the palms of destiny.
Every generation will
have to fend for itself,
we are told.
Those who know of
this oil in the sun
can attest to its color.
The grass is not only
greener where
the seasons are blessed.
Mangoes do not fall
where trees have
no leaves.
It is out of the goodness
of the heart that
a bountiful harvest
is assured the ardent farmer

and his presumptuous guest.
Let us wipe our sweaty foreheads
with the song of faith,
knowing with absolute certainty,
everything good will come,
like Sefi said.

Let the poor forget their sorrow

Sorrow plagues the poor
where the appetite for song
has drained peace with bitterness.

Who blames the sun,
if it delays its coming
to sing for the song-free heart?

Who blames the rain,
if it falls endlessly and
the harvest is postponed?

There are hearts
running errands to places
that lack company.

There are eyes vexed
by the distortion many celebrate
as the beauty of living.

Sorrow plagues the poor
where the appetite for song
has drained peace with bitterness.

Riff in the whirlwind

for Christopher Okigbo

bell ringer
gong striker

who knows the tale knows
what cap fits the teller

riff trespassing distant whirlwind –
skinbag of songs never lacking of verse

moon that will surely
cross night again

you…
 the singing ankle
 in the marketplace
you…
 the piper who put down
 the pipe to praise the gun

echo in the palm grove
oilbean wet
in rain free season

idoto's eyes, ogbanje
nwa loru uwa abo♣
who comes and leaves
as he wishes

these paths await your plod
now the gleam over earth's limb

♣ Igbo for child of two worlds

Remembering GB

They came for him that morning,
the seven soldiers armed, breath
smelling of weed and *kai-kai.**
His father, poor old man, set down
the newspaper, squinting
to see the strangers dressed in camouflage,
koboko whips in hand,
making straight for the back of the house.
His son's wild cry
seconds after they removed his teeth with pliers
and stripped him naked
in his bedroom,
almost left the old man with a weak heart.
Then they marched the young man they came for
to the rusty green jeep packed
on the street.
A great crowd watched,
keeping their distance from
the men in khaki
who hardly said a word but kept
their eyes on the watch.
His mother, hurrying home from
the market where she sold fresh tomatoes,
kicked her foot against a stone and
stumbled twice, at a loss for speech.
His sister, abandoning the *akara**
frying on the pan in the kitchen,
screamed and went after the jeep
but was restrained by neighbors.
Only the dust clouds after the blasting tires
retained the last look on GB's face,
the teardrops that betrayed him,

---

* local gin

* fried bean cake

bound, beaten, and bleeding
in the face.
News of his execution
in a graveyard unknown would
spread like wildfire the next day.
Who did not know
of the seven feet giant everyone
called Idi Amin, the lord of the streets
who took and bedded any girl he wanted
when he stood at the door of Empress Theatre,
Port Harcourt's movie magnet
to collect money from
any face he thought worthy of his intimidation.
But bullies always pay the price of karma
the hard way.
Five counts and four bullets was all it took,
according to the word in the town,
after the men in khaki had him
shovel his own pit
while they smoked weed and
passed round the bottle of *kai kai.*
All because he had touched
the sacred daughter and must now pay
to serve as a lesson.

Elephant grass

They are dancing;
The wind is laughing;
The goats shall have
the last laugh.

Ode to Akalaka[*]

I hear the heart
is unending
like a river.
That's been
your legend.
You came
to me last night,
speaking
in parables
voiced by
lightning distant.
Too afraid of light,
I retreated to bed.
In my sleep
I saw you
holding a machete
and 17 stones,
standing over
a river, dark
as a crow.
Your chants were
strange like
the mumbles
of an ancient god.
Yet I read in your eyes
the penetrating song
that fathered
the land of my birth.
If history were a paddle,
I would row across
the Orashi

---

[*] Mythical creator/founder of the Ogba people of Nigeria's Niger Delta region

to dress you
in a chiefly garment.
Embattled are
the fanfares
in the heart now,
the glow for your shadow
that stalks the fields at night,
invoking the dew drier
in the quiet realm
of night's passion.

For whom do we chant?

The coconut is open. Who
found the rope that hanged the tortoise?

Uwa ku la ka, Uwa ku la ka[*]

Handshakes are daggers. Do
you know a scabbard is naked when hands clasp?

Uwa ku la ka, uwa ku la ka

A smile is a riddle.
Read it carefully
so you don't get lost in interpretation.

Uwa ku la ka, uwa ku la ka

Every dawn is an elegy. Ask dusk
why there's so much sorrow in its eyes.

Uwa ku la ka, uwa ku la ka

Let the children wrestle
with the notes of the morning sun.
The moon shall teach them the wisdom in melodies
come nightfall.

Uwa ku la ka, uwa ku la ka

---

[*] Ogba for the world has spoken/universal wisdom